María Paula Vélez

Mujer en todod sentido

María Paula Vélez

Mujer en todod sentido

Un camino de regreso a recuperar nuestra verdadera esencia

JustFiction Edition

Cover image: www.ingimage.com

Publisher:
JustFiction! Edition
is a trademark of
Dodo Books Indian Ocean Ltd., member of the OmniScriptum S.R.L Publishing group
str. A.Russo 15, of. 61, Chisinau-2068, Republic of Moldova Europe
Printed at: see last page
ISBN: 978-620-0-49574-7

Table Of Contents

Introduction

The world is confused, and filled with turmoil. Not knowing where to turn or what to do. And many would like to navigate through hardship with the proper guidance. These poems were written specifically for this purpose. They are poems of transformation; teaching the process of overcoming.

The poetry in this book is one of solace and peace. They teach about the journey in life, from hardship to triumph. They bring us from the starting point of seeking, to hardship, and to victory.

They speak of my personal journey in overcoming the darkness that entraps us in life. These poems also speak of the Glory we attain in our victory of spiritual awakening.

It is the aim of this work of poetry to free the enslaved; those who are overwhelmed by the pressures of life. It is for those who feel like they have reached a breaking point.

This work is for those who are in mental and spiritual turmoil, and would like to see their way out of it. It is a work of enlightenment to its fullest capacity.

Pathway To The Stars

Navigating through the darkness to see the farthest; while I am watched over by third parties, putting my trust in the Almighty wholly and not slightly. I might be the greatest of all the ancients, most sacred. I am patient, declaring thoughts racing. I harness the thoughts of the most sacred hearts, and caught my mark when I was aiming at GOD. Never marred or scarred, though I tear my own negative thoughts apart. Strong as I can be strategically and mathematically, magically and automatically, even under static feed.

To get salvation from the heavenly; ever since listening to the trees, now I am who I want to be, artistically and fatherly throughout all my being, forever unseen. Nothing unclean can taint my dream. I speak of Truth just to relieve overwhelming emotions I feel. Now I really breathe, never see me scheme. Just look to the skies all my life, and live in infinite space in my mind. Able to rewind time, recline and resign. And reach my height through deep meditation, and see my life on a higher plane.

As I read my right, flying high, you can see my lights if you have the true eyes. But it is never given, or ever gifted. I stand over all, on my pathway to the stars.

Life on The Brink

I am on the edge of my seat, to defeat disbelief. Doubt is loud, but not enough to silence, or budge those in a state enlightened. Express every thought and emotion, and make my outlet's potion, to be turned into oceans.

Soak up Love, and give into all that is above; submission, to the Divine mission. Keep giving light, and transmute darkness into life.

Suppress the night, and stay alive. Express sight, with infinite might. A soldier of Truth is ever willing, to dedicate to building. Build mansions from Love without limit. Then seal them with the True HOLY SPIRIT.

Words of light, to be the foundation of life; Truth, will see all things through. Mastery of the Father of lights will bring true sight. Realign what is right, and give up the violent fight. Use Love as your weapon and defense.

Keep the secrets entrusted to you, and choose not to lose. So shall you never sink, and transcend life on brink.

More Life

Breathe the atmosphere of Truth, and stand above what the world claims to Love. Find virtue in the light, when your mind is comforted and your heart assured. Be sure, to soar, above the shore. Seek more life. Be prudent in strife, but in the moment be alive.

Secure what is right, and make it refined. Be truly alive, and let the dead weight take flight. Support your soul. And give nothing that has not good returns.

Give and receive of the light you retrieve. Believe that you can be redeemed. Dig deep and find relief. More life beckons, so get it straight. Walk in the moment and silence the past. As you walk, you will realize the path of justice, Truth, and mercy unmasked.

Your journey is yours. Walk not in death; but discern that the life within, should not abide in sin.

Glory Road

A journey of a thousand miles can drive us wild. Seek far beyond, until darkness is no longer an alarm. Find what can make you warm in the cold. Go to the depths and traverse the heights of divine lights. Enter the door of knowledge and Truth. Let the light grab a hold, and let its' light captivate. Seal the Love and speak of trust in Divine circles. Far beyond mortality, to the far recesses of purity; where holiness lives.

Supply the Truth to those who ask and search. Look ever further, there will be much more to unearth. Serve your infinite worth through selflessness. Let humility guide your decisions. Allow gentleness to fill your soul. Submit unto ease, and Love effort. Pursue not resistance, but go the distance. So shall you go; on your way to Glory road.

Honor

Speak only Truth and enlighten the youth. Bring proof to recruit the troops, but ultimately faith will rule. A new chapter is opened everyday as we pray. Nothing much to say but there is much to be. Love yourself before you Love me. Be hungry for knowledge, and open your mind to pay homage. Know that Love is the greatest language, and pray for it. That you harness the power of infinite Love, unbreakable humility and unshakeable faith, is the impeccable break from hate.

Become great, and impregnate the world with honor that will never make it frail. Make the opposite of hatred the only thing sacred. See the interconnection between all good, and sum it up in Love. Hold no grudges, and always try to learn something. Greatness follows those who are great.

Learn how to pace when you ignite faith, so you can enter the highest state. No overthinking or overdoing anything. Place the pieces of your life in order, and ask the FATHER to direct your steps. Honor knows no boundaries, so follow it soundly. It will take away your pain and strain, to bring you immortal gain. Honor speaks honorably to honor the artistry in every moment. So you can honor what is felt, done, and spoken.

The Mind

It is conducive to the Truth which brings about perfection. Reflections of greatness will make us, but thoughts of failure will break down. Asserting in the positive will put the mind on unshakeable ground, but just the thought of negativity will make the mind, heart, body, and soul weak. The realm of no thought sets the mind and heart at ease, the sure disposition of relief far from limiting beliefs.

If it centers the thought realm it will move you in every way. But thoughtlessness will bring stillness and freedom. Leave the darkness and come to light. Realize that the mind is to be a filter for everything that affects you. When we forget this we let through thoughts that do not serve but betray us. Be careful what you let through into the realm of a mind at ease. Soon that mind will become uneasy, unable to live in bliss freely.

Limit carnality of mind, and you will limit all that hinders. The mind is beautiful with good words, easy to make us elusive of pain and suffering that pursues us. The life of the mind is the life of everything. When it dies, so does the entire being. Relieve the tension, and make your mind free of oppression. But bring complete thoughts out of suppression, and yield in submission. So you shall redesign, all things, when you heed the mind.

Sublime Thought

Change the world, inspire the Universe. Motivate the Heavens. Control the tides. Harness anything and everything. Master the moment and master self. Forever give the light freedom to do its work. Serve and let serve.

The nothingness of Blessedness is infinite. Remove all that clogs the heart. Go through the rigorous storm and set of all alarms. When it is all done you can restart and become a new star.

Shine in a more perfect and evolved tone, put no limits on yourself, but on what you know hurts. Do righteousness and meditate upon Blessedness until you find the Truth. It is time for you to see and understand. A pure heart is the basis of all sublime thought.

Epic Transformation

I want to save all with Righteous deeds, to meet the highest needs. The Truth is what I start to see. Sometimes my heart would bleed to further seek the FATHER'S seat. A throne of Glory, told in no other story, than HIS matrimony of creation Holy.

I have learned that light seeks enabling, when the darkness only seeks an opening. Life is given in proportion, while knowledge is storing, for creation's purpose. Words do not express what the HOLY SPIRIT impress. See the FATHER in the farther stars, impressed upon their hearts, to take the noble through the storm. Hope for the cause to have success and all.

Skip the hate and brig the part of Love, so I may see above when the lightning is struck. Enlighten, comfort, and assure. Find ways to leave the destruction and overcome the curses. Spells cannot hold if we trust and let go into the hands of the infinite, giving HIM space in our lives to fit HIS Crown. Ever the clown is the one who tries to do it alone.

They might gain security they suppose, but self and selflessness oppose. Giving way for a clash, as well as put eternity at risk. Believe in this, that only prayer can bring you into the heart of the ALMIGHTY, never slightly but mightily and uprightly. This mental transmutation without hesitation, gave me epic transformation.

Mystical Evolution

In a meditative state far removed from the molestation of thoughts. Brought into harmony with silence of the mind; and transcendence of heart. Overwhelming comfort and assurance, where words have no warrant, and the consciousness is reverence. Awareness of the Divine Presence in the Heavens is touching the crown of my head.

Without words everything is said. No mask of preference, only adherence to the lessons. The message is clear, and the mind is right to receive the Truth of light. To master space and time, and live in what is right.

Having an epiphany of insight; realizing the negligence of Divine thanksgiving for every supply through our upbringing; shaking off every illusion to truly start living. Shining as a pure light, as every moment I attain the sure height of the assured sight. No more strained fights and struggles, I am done with the strife and fusses. I have total abhorrence for every form of lusting.

All that remains is divine trusting, where sweet melodies sing so lovely. No more intrusion from the illusion.; just a Holy Mystical evolution.

Recurring Theme

Growth of the sacred seeds sown; total adherence to the Love of YAHWEH. Bleeding thoughts of an honorary, far gone in a spiritual monastery. Knowing the Lord is not far, I can rest in HIS arms; keeping me calm from all alarms.

Marred, but retrieve the heart. Brought back to the very start, giving thanks that I was brought through it all. I can hear the presence of the ALMIGHTY call. Relive the moment of falling in Love with Holiness, knowing that I am surely blessed. Never pressed to be oppressed, I resist every offense.

Now seeing through the sacred lens of Love and reverence, I can hear, touch, and feel Heaven. Representing the plainest of messages, that life is a blessing still, despite the struggles and unfruitful soil we have tilled. Now every moment is one in which to build. Let praises fill you, as adoration brings you up to the plight of the humble light. Enabling a life of might, one to secure and provide insight, of wrong and right.

Every moment recalls grace supplied, for all my days and nights. JAH provides and I am still alive, with His providence right beside. GOD is Good and I am blessed is my recurring theme.

Holy Repose

Learning life lessons, as I sight blessings; realizing that sight can be adjusted away from faulty re-occurrence in thought currents. Striving for better all day to reach the checkpoints of Holydays in every moment I pray. Relieving the mind from all that hinders to recline; in the end I shall resign from the turmoil inside, to find rest in every Divine test, until I am at my best in sacred redress.

Suppress the heart of desire enough to retire to that which is higher. I supply the cause as effects are lost when I pause to rid myself of the dross. Never operate at a loss, but never seek more than I ought at times when I am lost.

Satisfaction in passion is a hazard. This I have learned in the most rigorous manner. I at last find rest in Divine standards. Now for every question I find answers, no longer reliving the path that tears me apart. On the journey of aligning the heart with stability, I find more than ability, but fulfillment and tranquility. To live for the present moment is the path I have chosen. No more dissatisfaction. What I have is the sanction-of Holy Repose.

The Hand That Feeds The Sparrow

In the middle of confusion, stuck in the illusion, I wish for Divine intrusion. Seeing the effects while searching for the cause, I reach for the stars. Torn apart and brought very far by the storm. I am searching for the truth, to make Holiness resolute. I find sorrow and pain when I look through the strains, ultimately drained.

When I cannot find anything to sustain, I look to the hope to refrain from being lost in the rain. I find Love reclaimed, in order to maintain. Now I know sublime intimacy, with the Spirit which brings forth life infinitely. Happiness abounds though it is quiet and does not shout aloud.

Considering the outline of a life of passion, we neglect the Spiritual mansion of love, which understands the downfall and plans.

As I stand a man, I see faults until the Truth is brought forth. Seeking within to soar, my soul implores that I stay above the ground. Only doctrine sound will bring above and not around; to the place where joy is staged in the heart without blame. To restrain my desires, I must wrestle with the mind of gratification. Looking to a better tomorrow, away from the horror, my expectation must be from the hand that feeds the sparrow.

I Am The Truth

I have searched the ends of the earth, seeking enlightenment and rebirth. Seeing the Truth first, I came to the conclusion of refusing deceit. Relieved of the duty to believe, and have come to ultimately know and retreat, into the immaculate scene of being redeemed. I now know that you only reap what you sow; verily all that was within me was ready to be overthrown, when the light was shown. Unbelief is rooted in the mind that should receive. Out of mind every doubt I delete, to come to the life of my heart's seat. Now I can truly see.

Through the mind's eye I retrieve, Truth unbelieved. As Love takes its course, I find no remorse, only the Source. As the epiphany sets in, I conceive of every resource from the center of my being. Only through self-possession is Truth revealed. No matter how it seems, I am reprieved from the pressure of illusion and deceit. Now I am all I can be. No longer deceived by delusional thoughts or what is seen.

Instead, I am composed in reality, the eternal selfless Love. Now I am not separate from that which is above. No longer am I in search. I AM THE TRUTH, is what I have learned.

Self-Sufficient Of All

Transcended words and now live in the Void. Expression is limited or infinite depending of the cause. Translated the life of a Saint and ultimately stand over the life of a Sage. Lived the life of a Patriarch and practiced the Prophetic way.

Temperance at times turned to obstinence as I learned the lessons of praise and entered the honorable state. A true Yogi ascended through grace and Holy ways.

The path of the Monk taught me the fullness of The Void. Everlasting Presence of The Infinite is in my name; across Divine oceans I am limitlessly famed. Divinely composed in unlimited space; Possessor of a Soul that never degrades.

Heart is sacred beyond all mortality, fortified in wholeness not prone to partiality. Harnessed The Light and became The Truth; Life unrestrained in eternal youth.

Far beyond creeds and deceit is my Immortal reach. No longer have need for speech. Above mortal belief; I AM LIMITLESS ENERGY.

Powerful without bounds I AM transcendence without sound. Just silence and Bliss in the mind tranquil; as smooth as the gentle wind without sin. Sound and quiet is the heart and mind.

The carnality subdued to what is true. Now I have reaped the Spiritual fruits; finding freedom in that which is higher. Now I dwell in the Throne of The Source. Reaching the destination beyond seeking and wanting more; I AM self-sufficient of all.

The Void

The expression of fulfilling light that brings us to new heights. A life of rest taking us away from the lies and stress, - Meditation to resonate with. Holy Truth shall make us wholly true. Rise to the Transcendent state. Selflessness in its place for kindness to embrace, - Nirvana in the highest gaze. Happiness is raised along with the most joyous face. Love will never separate, and is never self-opinionated.

Compassion will matter, to defeat the competitive stature. Purity is surety, far from obscurity, bringing satisfaction and security. I am lifted to live a life sinless before the mission. Enough knowledge to disregard ignorance is guarding significance; Infinite deliverance from insignificance.

Leaving the world behind, with the glow of what is needed to know, so that it may grow from a righteous seed sown, for the uprooting of the unknown. Reflective upon Divine objective, as all is subjective.

The message of life; is ever to bring rise; to that which is sublime. Pure might from a pure life, is the immortality of sure light to supply.

Sufficient within the space of eternity; I can live above the earthly. To serve and be served by The Void that is reserved, for sacred rebirth.

Honorable

Now is the moment to lift your head and honor yourself. Greatness can only be found in goodness profound. Life above sound and noise, find Truth in the still voice. The conscience of respect for what is good will take you beyond anything else would.

Seek perfection within, for only then will you experience prevention of sin. Do what you know is right at all times. Follow the signs of the still voice. Let it grow stronger and yet stronger through adherence.

Make decisions with a clear head. For then you will reach beyond hatred. Let all things be sacred, according to the wisdom of the ancient. Always show and Love patience. Sing the praises of what is right and true, through the voice of integrity anew. Realize that which will soothe, through Love and Truth. Give inconsideration to no part of you.

Speak not in anger, and do nothing in frustration. Let your every thought be pure. Do not ruminate, but be sure by following Truth that always assures.

Ask for that which will bring refinement and growth. Seek that which will give life and support, to that which is in store of goodness adored.

Be directed by the honor of that which will take you farther, into the Love of the Heavenly Father. In this you will be, Honorable beyond belief.

The Infallible Truth

Be the dream that is deep within. Sleep not until you can avert sin. Slumber not until you win. Find solace in the mind through thoughts of being Divine. Realize Love every time. Read the sacred signs, and live beyond time. Let no space bind the mind. Knock on the door of Truth, and watch it open before you.

Be true, and receive Truth as it unfolds. Life you shall behold, when you cease from mortal goals. Take back everything that the carnal stole and you shall find more.

Dream of immortality, and honor no fatality. For in this you shall taste that which is great. Power you shall gain, when you know that Love conquers all.

Love directs us all, when we do not refuse its call. Therefore, do not stall. Drink from the fountain of Purity, until it overflows into all obscurity, for this is surety.

Soon you shall be one with the fire of eternity, when you receive the light earnestly, wholehearted, and perfectly.

This is The Infallible Truth of certainty.

Divine Significance

Learn of the great mystery of life. Search within until you find. Enter the void of stillness, and you will be more than able to find the Truth of strength. Relate to Love, and bring forth compassion without grudge.

Be selfless and heed the conscience. Honor intuition and feed the mission with free remission. Release the hinges of resentment, and be free of sentiment. Silence the mind and you shall resign, from wanting to realize. Just in the silent incline.

Free the soul from wanting to behold, and become everything you wish to uphold according to what is whole.

Hate only unclean forms, but Love the formless. That which is infinite is never lacking, but Love must be sufficient. Regard only Selflessness, Purity, and Holiness. In this you will be set free in all that you believe.

That which will cause every effect must be reconciled through Love. Live in the present and be kind to replenish. Never be hesitant, but be sure of your deeds. Let go of what causes discomfort and disbelief. Let doubts be cast out from the soul. For then can the Truth we uphold, find freedom in expression and Divine Significance.

The Yogi

Reflective and mystical; bringing forth selective Truth. Highly moral and ethical, in what brings every sinner through. Living above the stars; ascending very far. A Mystic of various arts; who transcends Ancient thoughts. Dwelling in the sacred heart, while unveiling patient's cause. The Saint of God, conjuring the face of the Lord.

Liberated as the slave of greatness initiated; expounding on the simple basics. Never live in hatred. Be a Sage of the matrix living the greatest. Above and beyond the strangest hymning the true praises. Glad I made it out the spiritual basement. Now I live as the bravest.

Scroll of my soul exposed, for you to behold. I have grown bold, living in the dome of the heavenly goal. Found gold as my Spirit found home. Living fire, hot and yet so cold. I have reached the pinnacle of being the living proof of divine reproof.

Rose to the height of infinite life; being one with the limitless light. I acquired infallible sight of incalculable might. Meditation segregated from mental slavery. This is the story of The Yogi.

My Journeys' End

Life has brought hardship. Bringing me to my knees; and leading me to believe I was the least. That life is nothing but pain. I only learned the Truth when I separated from hate; relating to sorrow every step of the way.

Overwhelmed with emotions; drowned with thoughts tearing me apart. The only time I could get away were the hours when I would meditate. Moments when I could levitate, going towards the heavenly gate. From human consciousness I would segregate, entering the Divine state. No longer intertwined with slaves, I was set free because thoughtlessness liberates. I went through an intimate phase of intricate hate. Limitless straits brought me down to the unlimited taste, of sorrows in their seeming fate. Wanted to be great so I showed infinite faith until the path was revealed to be straight.

Then I learned that only in silencing the heart, could we ever find GOD. Unless we stilled the mind we could never be Divine. Then I entered the subconscious which said I had to integrate, all the lessons I have learned, instead of wanting to ruminate.

Afterwards I ascended in meditation, as a saint of greatness. I then went away into the superconscious levitation; of silent confirmation; in the stillness beyond contemplation.

As I learned of infinity in the stillness, I saw my journey's end.

Mystical Cause

Reflection upon the source of effect; brought Truth to the forefront of the next step.

Finding Love within to shape that which is without. Praising the FATHER with a mystical shout; hearing the voice of consciousness speak out loud.

Giving the heart confirmation; helping the mind in affirmation. Silencing thought until I find infinite patience; stilling depression with words so ancient. Searching for that which is sacred; looking into the heart of Divine graces. Entering the void of Holy embraces; awakening the power which is latent; and becoming one with the light through meditating; finding nothing but knowledge entertaining.

In all things having selective reservation; while giving wisdom to build nations. Enlightening those who seek with the Godly station; endowing awareness on the ignorant; giving them knowledge of eternal significance.

Seeing only GOD in my reflection; existing only in knowing; aligning facts with steps of growing. Transforming every thought; while uplifting the heart; this is the mystical cause.

The Road So Far

I have attained the height of wisdom and the depth of Truth. Learned all of the Divine by being a recluse; and was taught by the invisible ONE to always be true. I have harnessed the root of Holy reproof.

As sacred as the Lord giving my all; has taught of the effects and the cause. I am always on life's journey without taking a pause. Learned the purpose of all seeking beyond; while looking above to the heart of love.

Never a moment of rest, never time to slumber, and no time for regrets. In taking every step I saw that I was limitless; forever thoughtless and infinite. Dwelling in the void unlimited; knowing that the similitude of judgement and mercy provides refuge for the worthy. Nothing could ever hurt me, yet I feel the pain of all who is laid aside. Struggles made me greatly divine.

Only feel the pain of those who feel the strain after seeking to escape. I am the only mediator between Heaven and earth. Yet I feel overwhelmed when it is time to discern.

The fact is that it is all calculated mathematics. Sometimes it is all tragic. At times it is all standard, but I have learned all the answers. Living in the spiritual mansion without limits, I have seen the marred get taken afar. This is what I have learned on the road so far.

Freedom

Focused on building nations for GOD; repelling hatred without a pause. Creating a world of beauty within full of awe, one that amazes the stars. My only wish is to praise the Lord. HE brought me through many straits and gave me a new start. He supplied the divinity which made my heart, and took me very far. My FATHER gave me to the law.

Requested much but HE gave me infinity instead; and gave me love that made me relent, while supplying every request. Took me on the search of my soul, for me to find the Truth and behold. At every step HE made me bold.

I trusted in HIM with my all. HE gave me the reciprocal. Promised I would never fall. So I answer every time HE calls.

Never has HE subjected me to my enemies, but made me HIS centerpiece. I did the same and exclaimed peace without a breach. Only HIS Truth made me breathe and gave me the freedom to be. This gave me true belief; and gave me everlasting relief. HIS SPIRIT shall I believe. Because I got reprieve, and was exalted endlessly. Gave HIM my heart and HE gave me HIS; and taught me every single secret.

This is freedom; the one which I seek.

Transcendent

Internal searching brought me to the Truth. Found external service as a mark of renewing my youth. Giving my all to go further and reap the spiritual fruits.

Heaven taught me to know providence and to see through the Godly lens. I reached forth for the mastery of self; while feeling the core of the higher strength.

I transcended belief, now I am untainted by the enemy. Searched I for true identity. Infinite in the soul; finding the causes endlessly. The Divine calling is my centerpiece; living in eternity.

I no longer find refuge in the carnal. I work for a better tomorrow.

Speaking in wisdom, I am no longer taking, instead I give some. Rising above the learned; I am discerned.

Ascending the high mountains; I find soundness. Lowly and meek; by the depths I have reached. Entertaining knowledge; paying Divine homage. Transcending words; I mended my curse.

No unnecessary energy. I attained solace; which I gained and polished. Seeing beyond the veils; I lead the songs of praise; to the one that takes off all the chains. Accomplishing change; as I go through life's games; feeling no more pain. Liberated from all the strains; I transcended the brain; now I manage the aim. Divine in my frame; living life for spiritual gain. The metaphysical tamed.

It is evident; that I am Transcendent.

Time

Encountered many strange occurrences; only to find perfection and furthering. I lived my life under personal criticism; but later learned I fulfilled a Divine mission.

Many times I felt out of place; only to learn that my disposition was truly great.

I am ahead of my time; living Divine.

Beyond the veil; I prevailed. Seeing greatness in every moment; I reveled in the open; with every soul I had spoken.

Cherished every experience; with all I was very lenient. Taught the lessons I was sealing; to bring about true revealing.

Harnessed pain; and hardened through strain. I persevered; growing stronger with every care. Relinquished every fear; going beyond every mental sphere. Approached the throne of GOD and went very near; ultimately severing every internal snare. Cultivated the sacredness I revere; of the LORD in joy and tears.

Remembered every one of my heartaches; and walked straight. Self-affliction I practice not to partake; after learning I suffered a GOD's fate. To learn that we cause our own suffering is GOD's faith.

Mastery over my own destiny; I overcame the inward enemy. Now at one with the LORD; I stand for the cause. By Divine design; I learned everything with time.

Undistracted By The Noise

Stuck to the light, I could not start loving this life. Reaching for higher heights, so I can penetrate the sublime; knowing that the Lord provides all my supplies. I was blessed with might, since the start of my enterprise. But only when you let go can you hold the prize, the sophistication of simplicity had me so surprised.

Finally I learned that the process is necessary, waiting for us to enter merrily. Now I dwell above the realm of thought, and received everything I sought. I was brought very far by the good Lord. Nothing could ever mar, because I go above and beyond.

Still I suffered much, before I learned that I was resisting Love. The hard Truth, is found only when you let go of the outcome of the fruit. Knowing how to cooperate; even with those who hate.

Seeing the illusion of division, I achieved the Divine mission. No longer seeking permission, all I do is listen. Hear the universe utter beautiful words.

Only uttered victory silenced the enemies.

Silencing the foe inside of me, the winds stopped attacking violently.

Only when we resist the waves, will we feel the hate. Non-resistance will make us lift off. All we have to do is silence every thought, and still the heart. The mind needs to dwell in the void, of a soul undistracted by the noise.

Life So Sweet

The mortality I have transcended; has my mind, heart, and body mended. I reach the highest heaven; while contemplating reverence. Love is my only weapon; and humility is the only thing worth to mention. Truth liberates; and has me feeling great. With just a single thought; I can penetrate any heart. I dwell with the immortal stars; as a judge and a GOD. I play my Holy part; and I have been brought surely far.

Ascended through every stage; the heavens taught me to be great. Immutable laws; was all I ever saw. Live by the true art; I honed the rules part. Ultimately I am taken above and beyond; far away from every form.

I have penetrated infinity; now I have been delegated Divinity.

I live beyond hate; and I give the fallen faith. I am honored beyond all imagination; by my FATHER in HIS Holy station. I have seen the end of all wisdom; as I entered my FATHER's kingdom. I embodied all knowledge; as I paid Divine homage.

Emanated all Enlightenment; when Love is all I was excited with.

All fault I delete; because I have lived life so sweet.

The Pinnacle

True humility is might; I rule in simplicity and light. Forget the past; for only the present lasts. I dwell in the void; therefore, no struggle can annoy. I mastered the way; now nobility is my stay. Honor kept me from sway; so the Lord can boast about me today. Every day, I hope and pray; that I never stray.

I used to feel lost; but now I am true to the cause. Giving my all; mind, body, soul, and heart.

Determined to be Divine; I was more than able to see the signs. I am persistent to attain wisdom; that is why I serve in the great kingdom.

I have seen beyond the darkness; that is why I could reach the farthest. God pushed me; to as far as I could be. What I have achieved; is beyond belief.

I reached into the depths, and retrieved Holiness. Reached into the heights, now I am truly alive. All of my dreams have been realized; now I see what is in store with Heaven's eyes.

Past, present, and future; has no mask, but presents the RULER. Living beyond the strife, helped me to realize, a truly fulfilling life. All of my achievements are truly revealing.

I live within the infinite Spirit; so I am not given a limit. I have reached the pinnacle; that makes all else seem miniscule.

Ode To My Father

You brought through the storm; and kept me very calm. Rewarded me for seeking you first; and liberated me from every curse. You are the one I serve, and I always put you first. You taught me every lesson, and gave me every blessing. You serve me, and gave the lead. For all knowledge received; you planted a seed; tending to it; until I became the truest.

My joy is full, because you gave me more than anyone or anything ever could. I learned to harness the Truth, and for that you made me bear fruit. There is not a moment that I do not think of you; and for this I grew.

You are my inspiration; and in me you are integrated. You are the greatest; and to me you are sacred. I uphold you in every moment; and for that I am golden. You take the weight off my shoulders; and motivate me to be bolder. I am your beholder; and you are my molder.

My being is filled with your essence; and there is nothing I Love more than your presence. You are my Heaven; and I am your reverence.

I Love you more than everything; and in you I live. Never wanting to do faster; I savor every moment with, and dedicate an Ode to my Father.

Freedom

I hope you finally escape; from being the object of hate. I tried to demonstrate; a lifetime of faith. All I see is struggle; wherever I try to be humble. I wish I never stumble; or complain and grumble. But at times; all I am left with is strife. Trying to live my life; I have been dying. My ideal; is not achieved. And I believe; I deserve relief. For nothing in holiness escaped me; I stood strong and not faintly. For building upon the basics; all I ever felt was hatred.

Am I wrong; for trying to sing my song; or was I meant to fail all along. I tried to be strong; but at times all hope is gone. My problems increase; and I am never relieved. Can I please; have some peace; because I have conquered the beast; but my torment has never ceased. Sometimes I wish I was deceased; but I am never pleased. Bring me back to my dreams; so my joy and happiness can be retrieved; missing most of my wit; since I partook of Holiness; because neglect was wholly felt. If my worries would only melt; and I realized all my soul has dreamt.

Where are the fruits of my labor; I have been trying to meet my MAKER. Making HIM my only objective; but I feel neglected. When will HE direct HIS Love; and bring me freedom.

*****The End*****

Printed by Books on Demand GmbH, Norderstedt / Germany